D0312999

The Precious
Moments
Of
Our Lives

The Precious Moments Of Our Lives

by Angela Grace

Illustrated by Samuel J. Butcher

BALLANTINE BOOKS
NEW YORK

A Ballantine Book
Published by The Ballantine Publishing Group
© 2003 by Precious Moments, Inc.
Licensee: Random House Publishing. All rights reserved.

All rights reserved under International and Pan-American
Copyright Conventions. Published in the United States
by The Ballantine Publishing Group, a division of
Random House, Inc., New York, and simultaneously
in Canada by Random House of Canada Limited, Toronto.

Ballantine and colophon are registered
trademarks of Random House, Inc.

www.ballantinebooks.com

Library of Congress Cataloging-in-Publication Data
is available upon request from the publisher.

ISBN 0-345-45942-3

Book design by Julie Schroeder

Manufactured in the United States of America

First Edition: March 2003

10 9 8 7 6 5 4 3 2 1

*L*ife is made up of *precious moments*, and it is our memory of these moments that inspires us and reminds us what matters most—that life is a priceless gift to be cherished.

Sometimes trials and tragedies make us question our faith and the importance of our lives.

It is easier to be happy and content during good times, but during times of difficulty and struggle, faith and hope are especially necessary.

This is when our memories of *precious moments* rekindle the flame of past joys and strengthen us.

They fortify us in the face of adversity.

Sometimes it's a simple childhood memory or, perhaps, the recollection of a parent's love, or a baby's smile. Sometimes it's the warm presence of a close friend.

Our lives are filled with these treasures. They bring a smile to our lips, a lift to our spirits, and a bit of warmth to our hearts—and they are always there.

These are the *precious moments* of our lives.

*D*o you remember . . .

...when your mother
held you?

It was a long time ago, but that feeling of love is still
   with each of us today.

She was your first protector.

She nurtured you.

She brought you into this wonderful world.

She gave you unconditional love, and wanted nothing
   in return.

She was always there for you, and you never felt safer
   or more secure than when you were in her gentle
   arms.

...your first step?

You felt a wonderful combination of freedom and
excitement slightly tinged with fear and uncertainty
as you stood there. Then, with one slightly unsure
and unsteady lunge, you were on your way.

This was it.

You were on your own, barreling forward, and off to
see the world.

Yet you knew that a helping hand and a steady arm
were always within easy reach.

You weren't alone.

There was always someone there for support and
guidance.

It was only your first step, but it was also the start of a
great journey, and those who loved you were
there to share in your first great
accomplishment.

4

...when you first realized
how great the world
was and how you were
only a very small part of it?

You were awestruck.

You wanted to see it all but were daunted by the task.

At first you felt small. What were you compared to the
   great continents and the deepest oceans?

They were so big and you were so tiny.

But then you realized that you were no less than the
   seas and the mountains.

You, too, were a part of God's wonderful
   creation.

...your first special friend?

Maybe your friend was an older sister or brother, an aunt or uncle, or just a close friend of the family.

They were different from your parents.

They were special because you realized that they didn't have to like you the way your parents did.

They liked you because you were you.

You shared common interests, and they shared the wisdom of their experiences with you.

You both treasured your moments together, and they helped to make you a better person—the person you are today.

*...the first time you noticed
the wonders of the
world around you?*

The simple beauty of a flower.
The loving affection of a pet.
The immense beauty that surrounds you every day.
It was a lot to take in, and you probably spent hours
just staring at the wonders of nature.
Sometimes we become distracted by concerns both big
and small and may not notice the bountifulness of
life around us. During these times we can take
refuge in our memories of the past, memories
of discovery and wonder that allow us to
reexperience these marvels today.

...when baths were fun?

First they were playtime in water, something to look
    forward to with childlike delight.

Only later did they become the chore of getting
    clean—an unwanted interruption to the very
    important business of playtime.

Now, miraculously, you look forward to baths once
    again.

They are a moment to rest and relax, a sanctuary
    from the heated obligations of the day.

Warm water, soothing music, and a chance to get
    away from it all.

Once again baths are fun.

...your grandmother's love?

She had a special sort of love. She was always there to
fill in with the little things that occasionally your
parents might have missed: the perfect birthday
present, a freshly baked cookie, a warm lap to fall
asleep on.

She was the wisest person you knew, and probably
the most loving, and though she eventually was
called to heaven, the memory of her face
brimming with love is a constant source of
strength and encouragement.

...the first chance you had to
share something?

Perhaps you shared it with a new friend, not a mentor
or a teacher, just someone like you.

Maybe it was a game, a make-believe tea party for
two, a little bit of playtime imagining that was so
much more fun because it was shared with someone who was willing to play along.

And in that moment a friendship was born, and there
was nothing make-believe about it.

And you shared that bond of friendship between you
for the rest of your lives.

...the great seesaw of life?

Everybody has their ups and downs.

Sometimes you're happy and sometimes you're sad.

Things change, and sometimes you have to change with them.

Maybe you're not the one who is down. Maybe it's someone else whom you care about, and maybe you feel guilty about being up when they are down.

Sometimes life is like that. Sometimes we have to share the ups and the downs, the highs and the lows.

These times are all the more special because they are shared with someone else.

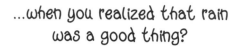

...when you realized that rain was a good thing?

Rain waters the gardens and feeds the soil and
fills the reservoirs so that we have plenty of
cool, clear water to drink.

Though a storm might sometimes upset
our outdoor plans, it is nonetheless God's
will and he knows best.

He also provides us with shelter from the storm,
whether under an umbrella or within the confines
of our warm, dry homes.

We know the rain will pass, and the world will be a
better place for it.

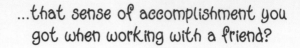

...that sense of accomplishment you got when working with a friend?

Maybe you did a bit of sewing, or
   baked a batch of chocolate-
   chip cookies on a wintry
   afternoon.
Maybe you did something
   as simple as building
   a sand castle together.
Just the two of you working together,
   making something special.
And in the end, the warm feeling
   of a shared accomplishment
   was more meaningful
   than the accomplish-
   ment itself.

...when you held your memories in your hand?

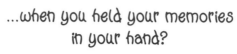

You had a diary, and you kept all of your deepest
secrets and thoughts in it.

Everything you felt seemed so much more real
because you could read it on the page.

It was the story of your life, and as you kept filling
the pages, you would sometimes go back and read
passages again.

You were amazed and proud of all you'd accom-
plished. And you couldn't wait to find out how the
story ended. You would write that down too, later,
on the blank pages that were yet to be filled.

The pages set aside for your future.

...when you began to wonder what lay ahead?

Should you go to college, get a job, move to another
    city, maybe start over?
There were so many choices.
You thought, *If only I had a crystal ball, if
    only I could see what the right choices are,
    if only I knew how it all turned out.*
The future is a mystery to us, but that is OK.
Life is meant to be experienced one day at a time.
God knows what the future holds for us.
All we need to remember is that we are always in His
    more-than-capable hands.

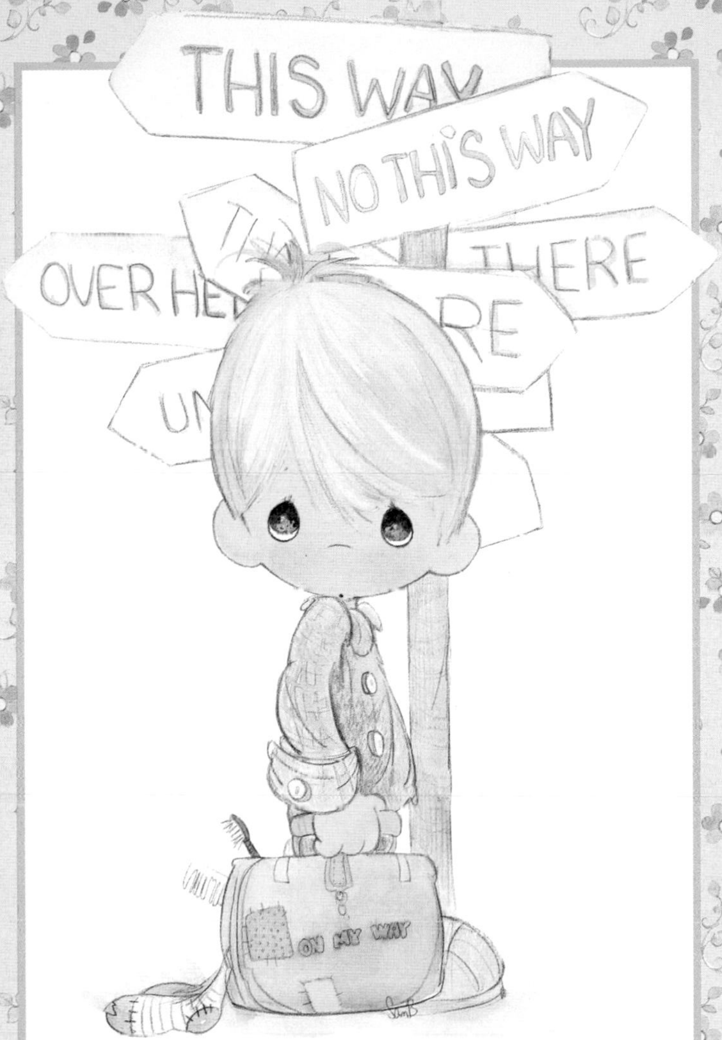
THIS WAY
NO THIS WAY
THERE
OVER
ON MY WAY

*...when you realized that,
just by being yourself,
you were good enough?*

Even the best of us sometimes succumb to peer
pressure.

What others think about us or say behind our backs
should never be the measure by which we judge
ourselves.

It is impossible to please everyone or meet their
differing expectations.

Trends and styles constantly change. What's trendy
today could be tomorrow's bargain basement.

What matters most is who we really are, and that's the
way God wanted it to be.

Being one's self is good enough for anyone, and it
never goes out of style.

...the first time you appeared before an audience?

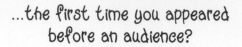

You had practiced for many weeks, and you were
    finally ready.
Then you were on the stage and in the spotlight and
    all eyes were upon you.
Sure you were nervous, but you had rehearsed and
    this was your moment.
The audience applauded, but, more important, you
    knew that you had done your best.
Your performance may not have been on Broadway or
    in the Olympics or televised from coast to coast.
None of that was important.
All that mattered was that you had done your best.
You deserved their applause.

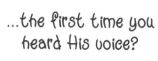

...the first time you heard His voice?

It didn't come over the radio or the television or even
by telephone.

You might have been alone or with a lot of people.

Where it happened wasn't important.

The good Lord spoke to you from within, and where
you were or what you were doing didn't matter.

He was always there from the day you were born,
whispering encouragement and offering guidance.

Sometimes we might overlook His wisdom or ignore
His advice.

None of us is perfect.

But He doesn't go away.

He is always there.

All we have to do is listen and heed His word.

*...the thrill of being part
of something
larger than yourself?*

Maybe you were playing on a team or in a band or
performing in a play.

Maybe you were just lending your voice and cheering
enthusiastically to encourage those who were
actually participating.

Even if you were only on the sidelines, wasn't it great
to be a part of things?

Their victory became your victory, because in the end
we are all in this together.

We are never alone, and every win is shared by all.

...graduation day?

Your formal schooling was over, and your classes
behind you. You'd turned in your assignments,
and completed your tests.

Graduation day had arrived, and you had earned
your degree.

Everyone was so proud of you as your name was
called out, and you received your diploma.

But more tests were still before you, the tests of
everyday life where you applied what you had
learned over so many years.

You were a graduate, the hope of the future—and
you were ready to do your part.

...the first time you led the way?

It was exciting and maybe it was scary, and the person with you was younger and more uncertain than you.

You had to lead the way, not just for yourself but for your youthful charge as well.

You were older and more experienced, and you knew that the two of you were not alone.

...the first time you were out on your own?

You had left home, confident and self-sufficient and ready to take on the world.

You were your own person, an adult, your own boss for the first time in your life.

What new opportunities awaited you—excitement, adventure, opportunity, and wonder.

It was all very thrilling.

It was all very liberating.

You were on your own.

But you knew that you weren't really alone. Home was still there, back at the beginning of the road along which you'd come—and you traveled on.

...the beauty of music?

You sat down and you played it, your fingers gently
finding the keys.
There it was; you were making beautiful music.
It was your song.
Your gift to all of those around you.
Someone else might have written it and played it
before you did, and others might be able to play
it more beautifully than you, but no matter.
The music was beautiful and you were a part of it.

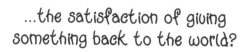

...the satisfaction of giving something back to the world?

Toil and sweat can actually be pleasant and enriching
when they are for a good cause.

Giving back is good, and sharing the bounties
of one's harvest with others is another way of
celebrating the blessings that we have had
bestowed upon us.

Lending a neighbor a helping hand, performing a
bit of community service, or even doing your small
part to conserve nature are all ways of making the
world a better place.

And when the world is a better place, we all feel good
about ourselves and the world.

...the feeling of
being well prepared?

Your backpack was full, everything had been checked,
and you were ready to go.

No one could know what lay ahead, but you weren't
afraid.

You were well prepared for any foreseeable situation,
rain or shine.

True, there was always the possibility of the unexpected.

But you weren't really alone.

Even in the wilderness you would never be
abandoned.

...the first time you
realized that the grass
might not be any greener
on the other side
of the fence?

Sometimes we become distracted by little details,
and compare ourselves to others. Things might
look better from afar, maybe fresher and more
desirable—but that is not the whole picture.
When you look at things more closely, you realize that
there is no reason for envy.
What you have is enough.
Contentment lies in the realization that the greatest
bounty is within each of us.

...the first time you noticed the change of the seasons?

It was harvest time, and summer had come to an end.

The leaves were all turning, and you knew that soon the ground would be covered in snow.

Winter was coming.

God made the way of the world in a never-ending cycle of seasons that mirrors our lives—the cycle of birth, life, and death.

The seasons are another symbol of the path we all must take.

We too shall return to life after we have died, no different from the crops of last summer that await rebirth under their protective blanket of snow.

...when you met that
special person with whom
you would share your life?

First it was an exchange of looks, then of words, and
then of time: moments and gifts shared without
regret.

Maybe it was an awkward beginning.

Relationships can be as fragile as flowers, delicate and
easily damaged, a beautiful array of pretty petals
and sweet perfume.

Like flowers, relationships are gifts to all of the senses,
a living bounty of blessings.

But unlike flowers, your love was not temporary.

It was forever.

Both of yours, shared together.

...that first special dish you prepared?

You liked to cook, especially all of your favorites.
But this meal was different.
Maybe it was something simple, a dish you had made
　　hundreds of times before.
Maybe it was something unique, a family tradition,
　　or a new recipe you'd never tried before.
It might have been just a batch of cookies, or a full-
　　course meal that took hours to prepare.
What mattered most was that you'd made it for
　　that special someone, and that you shared it
　　together.

...when that
special day came?

You said, "I do."

A covenant was made.

You were married, and two became one.

You were dressed in white and he was handsome and tall.

You danced together and shared your joy with family and friends.

It was like starting on yet another journey, taking a new road—but this time you were not alone.

You were with someone.

Someone who would be there always and forever.

*...the first time you
looked back and realized
how much time had passed?*

You hadn't always been together, but it sure felt like
you had.

The memories you'd created together seemed greater
than the memories of all that came before.

These *precious moments* together only strengthened
you for the future that awaited you both.

The good, the bad, the times of joy and the times of
sadness.

Memories to be shared together, even more meaningful because they now belonged to both of you.

...the most precious gift that you gave each other?

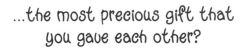

It came from your love, a blessing from God.

A new human life!

Baby seemed so defenseless.

So helpless.

You had to care for Baby.

Love Baby.

Both of you together.

Bringing Baby into the world might have been difficult, but any hours of pain and discomfort quickly faded away as those little eyes opened and looked at you.

Little eyes filled with love for both of you.

Baby was the child of your love, God's greatest blessing for parents.

Remember how you felt the first time you held that loving little bundle in your arms?

Your world changed forever and was filled with love.

...when your house became a home?

It didn't happen overnight.

Like houses, homes have to be built from the ground up.

A solid structure on a stable foundation followed by gallons of paint and rooms full of furniture.

So it was with your home.

Your love was the stable foundation.

Your marriage the solid structure.

Soon your marriage was filled with the products of your union: memories, family, and an unending supply of love.

A simple house had become a home.

...the little chores
that were all a part
of keeping the family happy?

Housework and laundry.

First to the washer, then to the dryer.

There were never enough clean clothes, and the piles
kept growing.

It was an effort just to keep up.

It could be discouraging.

And then you turned around and there was a little
one pitching in to help, and all of a sudden things
weren't so overwhelming.

You were all in this together.

These were family chores.

All a part of making a house a home.

...when you realized that you were indispensable?

Your family relied on you.

Not just for the cooking and the cleaning or the
  paycheck or the transportation to here and there.

They needed you for that special something only
  you could provide.

Yours were big shoes to be filled.

And then one day your little one was playing dress
  up and stepped into your shoes (those big shoes),
  and you realized that there were shoes even bigger
  than yours.

And that was OK because the good Lord was always
  there to fill them.

...the first day of school?

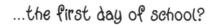

No, not your first day, your child's.

You were now the mother, and it was time to share your bundle of joy with the rest of the world.

Sure you were worried. Maybe you were even more worried than when it was *your* first day.

You thought for a moment.

"This must have been how *my* mother felt."

The memories of her fortified you.

You had to be brave.

This was a big step for your child, one that you were sharing—and one that your child in turn would share with their own child in the future.

Just like you had with your mother.

...when you realized that life was full of surprises?

Life is a gift to be cherished.

Sometimes we are distracted by the pretty bow or the colorful wrapping.

Sometimes we set our hearts on the contents, anticipating something that may or may not be there.

Sometimes there are disappointments, but these usually come from our own false expectations.

Life is to be experienced here and now.

Joyful surprises are part of the gift. They're even more special because they are unexpected.

DO NOT
OPEN TILL
CHRISTMAS

...when you first recognized
all of the blessings
that surround us each day?

Some blessings are big and life altering—finding true
love, having a baby, or finding the house of our
dreams.

Other blessings might be easier to miss or take for
granted—a sunny afternoon after a week of bad
weather or a kind word when you need it most.
Even a basket of newborn puppies whose only
desire is to spread joy and happiness.

We should be grateful for all our blessings, however
big or small.

...that real peace
in our world
is possible?

It is easy to get discouraged in these trying times.
Sometimes the problems and struggles people face the
    world over can be overwhelming.
But it's important never to lose hope because one day
    the world will be at peace.

...when you noticed all
of the people around you
who had dedicated their
lives to helping others:
the firemen, the policemen,
the doctors, and school teachers
who work tirelessly to make
the world a better place?

Some just devote their time.

Others risk their lives with no thought for their own
safety.

Everyone has to do his part.

We are all in this together.

...the first time you contemplated the heavens above?

There were so many stars, so many far-off worlds that they all looked like twinkling little lights on some holiday decoration.

The universe is so big it boggles the mind.

As if our world wasn't big enough, you wondered where you fit in the great expanse of the galaxies.

The answer is simple. Right where you are currently standing.

You have a right to be here. You are needed and important.

You are part of the universe as well.

...your many Precious Moments?

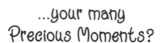

Where did all of the time go?

Yesterday, you were held in your mother's arms.

You took your first step.

You set out on your own.

You found that special person.

You built a life together.

Life is a book with chapters of *moments* that we experience one page at a time.

It is good to pull out the old album and look back at these pages. They can provide comfort in times of trouble and strife.

Memories are all the more special when they are shared with someone special.

The *precious moments* of our lives.

Indeed all of our lives are made up of precious moments.

They are the little gifts from God that make our lives worth living.

In times of trouble and strife we take comfort in memories of these moments.

They are the bits of joy and solace that aid us through life's difficulties and times of sadness and sorrow.

God is with us always, and our live's *precious moments* are His most blessed gifts to us.

 *Angela Grace*